an infatuations notebook

# The Quilter

Illustrations by Elizabeth Stewart
Cover artwork Elizabeth Stewart
*a little quilt story* Illustrations by Penny Brown

Museum Quilts

My home is a quilt — each room a block. It is filled with fabric and needlework and loved fiber treasures made by hand, each reminding me of its maker. What good company they are. I am never lonely.
Betsy Nimock, USA

NOT A COMPLETE DISASTER THEN!

In the United States we can buy personalized license plates for our vehicles. I wanted to have plates that expressed my favorite pastime, so I ordered one that read 'I Quilt' for my car. I had not realized that when my husband drove the car people were questioning him about the plates, until he came home one day and announced that he was going to order a plate for his truck that would read 'I Don't'.

Shelly Burge, USA

Planned with joy, sewn with love,
This quilt was made for using.
Hid away with dust and creases
No cares, it would be soothing,
Use it, wash it
Perhaps 't'will need repairing
But thanks enough to me will be
The communion of sharing.

Jenni Dobson, Great Britain

If I were cast away on the BBC's *Desert Island*, swatches of fabric would be more comforting and evocative than eight discs.

Deidre Amsden, Great Britain, in *The Passionate Quilter* by Michelle Walker.

*Desert Island is a radio programme broadcast by the BBC. It invites personalities to imagine they are cast away on a desert island. Each is allowed to choose eight records to take along.*

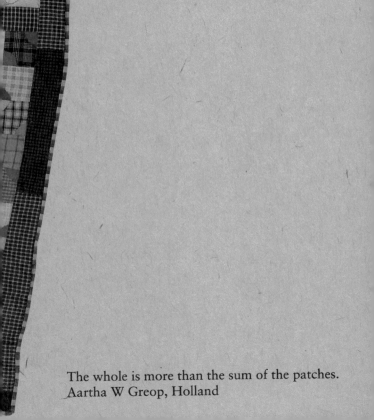

The whole is more than the sum of the patches.
Aartha W Greop, Holland

The abiding appeal of quilting is that it requires only basic skills and materials and yet the results can be extraordinarily beautiful — think of wholecloth quilts made from plain white cotton fabric and stitched with white thread. These quilts have an understated elegance and richness which belies the 'everyday' materials and stitches from which they were made.

Barbara Chainey, Great Britain

When buying a new car, a quilter takes a tape measure to check if the frame will still fit inside.
Overheard by Jenni Dobson, Great Britain

I bet there's not a single person who makes a quilt easily. You work at it. We work hard at it...lots of brain activity planning it, lots of muscle activity hauling fabric and equipment, and lots of finger activity cutting and stitching and ripping out and restitching to get it just the way we want it. No, making a quilt is not easy, but there's nothing that beats the pleasure we feel when we have clipped off the last thread end, and our very own quilt, child of our heart, is finished.

Helen Kelley, USA

Don't be the one to die with the most fabric — use it and enjoy it while you can.
Anon

We have a very nice tradition in our group, Blockhaus-Quilter Wien, in which there are 24 women and one man. Each member gets for their 'round birthday' (eg, 30, 40) from each of us the same signed friendship-block, the batting and the backing and must finish the quilt herself. In the first year we had to make ten blocks, the following year three, last year none and this year three. It is fun and we have many lovely results.
Hanna Afritsch, Austria

Q is for Quilting, Q is for Quiet time, Q is for Quality in workmanship and friendship.
Carter G Houck, USA

The quilters dilemma: How can I find more time? I practice the 'Monet Method'. He kept a canvas in progress for different times of the day and since my ancestors are related to Claude Monet, this makes it legal for me to have at least three to four projects going at one time. It's a healthy approach that results in the gradual completion of many quilts. One has to believe Creative Clutter Tops Idle Neatness.
Georgia J Bonesteel, USA

'The patch collector'

Whilst studying quilting designs, especially feather wreaths, I took a country walk with a male colleague. There were some large birds' feathers laying on the grass on our route so I picked them up to draw later. I explained they were for a quilt project I was working on. My friend was puzzled. 'Won't it take a few more than those to stuff a quilt?' he inquired!

Jill Crawley, Great Britain

Earth quilts are my silent voice joining the choir of women worldwide, singing a universal language of love and the beauty of patchwork, while expressing their heartfelt desire for peace, social and environmental justice.

Meiny Vermaas-van der Heide, Holland

I was helping to sell fabric remnants at a quilt show. During the day a woman in a wheelchair made many visits to the stall. Each time I rummaged and turned over the pile picking out treasures for her. As the show finished she made yet another visit. I was busy and could not help her. To my amazement she arose from her chair and was in there with the best of them!

Irene MacWilliam, Ireland

I had made a piece of work on an aquatic theme. Attached to it were lots of strings of small fish. I carried it in to the exhibition hall past a man cutting the grass. As I handed it in I noticed I was one string short. I went outside and discovered it had gone through the lawnmower. Among the grass clippings I found twenty fish which I reattached to a new cord. Several weeks later among the dried grass cuttings I found more fish and a complete but much stained cord.
Irene MacWilliam, Ireland

'The origins of rotary cutting'

Quilters stitch friendship together in their quilts.
Atsuko Ohta, Japan

I discovered quiltmaking in 1989 and one of the first things that I was told was to 'Consider colour and design before worrying about technique, good technique will come with time.' If, in the beginning, I had been made to produce a sampler quilt, then I would not have abandoned my well-paid career to study for an Art Degree. Perhaps there is something to be said for sampler quilts after all!

Colin Brandi, Great Britain

Quilting has often been described as 'pick-up' work; I
describe it as a pick-me-up.
Anon

Standing is stupid, crawling's a curse.
Skipping is silly, walking is worse.
Hopping is hopeless, jumping's a chore.
Sitting is senseless, learning's a bore.
Running's ridiculous, jogging's insane.
Guess I'll sit down to my quilting again.
Sheila Scawen, Great Britain

Sweatshirt seen at US quilt show bearing the words 'My husband said he'd leave me if I bought any more fabric — I sure do miss him!'

1990

The following lines from a poem by T S Eliot, from *Four Quartets*, which I embroidered on the back of the first quilt I made, conjure up much of what quiltmaking means to me:

> Here between the hither and farther shore
> While time is withdrawn, consider the future
> And the past with an equal mind.

These lines bring to mind two aspects of quiltmaking, both the meditative state of being suspended in time that accompanies the process of quiltmaking for me, and the bridge that the quilts themselves form between past, present and future.

Marilyn Henrion, USA

The first time I picked up two pieces of fabric to begin making patchwork, I little realised what it would lead to. From an absorbing hobby to an obsession, it developed into a new career. One that has given me the opportunity to travel widely and provided a network of friends both in the UK and abroad. Many of my quilts are developments of the traditional pieced patchwork patterns and my aim is to preserve and maintain those design elements whilst giving them a contemporary feel, thus linking the past and the future in this living craft.
Katharine Guerrier, Great Britain

Look at a red poppy, then turn your eyes on to a white wall and a green poppy appears. In the same way, green grass becomes reddish if you quickly turn your eyes to a white summer cloud.

To look East from West you may discover the two are complimentary.

Yoshiko Jinzenji, Japan

Ah quilting! The mere mention of the word conjures feelings of love, security, warmth and great joy!
Nancy Johnson-Srebro, USA

Every tradition we have belongs to the current generation, but only as trustees, in other words we are caretakers and we have a duty to our tradition to take it and be faithful to it. But we must also enrich it to the extent that it has passed through our time and we have a duty to pass it on in that new, refurbished form to the next generation.

Annette Claxton, Great Britain, from Father Pat Ahearn on the subject of traditional Irish dance

Patchwork and quilting always travel with me. Once, when our plane was diverted from Gatwick to Scotland, I continued to work on my current project. As we waited for information, my husband turned to me, saying 'You are the calmest person in this aircraft.'.
Gillian Clarke, Great Britain

Quilts have brought me many things. But the most precious one is many wonderful friendships.
Atsuko Ohta, Japan

There are so many colours and fabrics available to quilters today. When looking for fabric use your eyes, search for the unusual, take a risk, create a surprise, enjoy yourself and have fun. For an exciting quilt it is better to use 4 inches of one hundred fabrics than 100 inches of four fabrics.
Jennifer Hollingdale, Great Britain

One day I decided to experiment with coloring fabrics. I wanted to create unique designs but I forgot to wear protective glasses and a mask. After mixing powdered dyes with water, I hung pieces of wet muslin fabric over a fence and began spraying and splashing dyes on them I even took pinches of the powdered dye and sprinkled them on the fabric. They were looking great until my husband came home and asked me what was wrong with my eyes? The dust from the powders had dyed my plastic contact lenses, they were bright purple.
Shelly Burge, USA

Make as many quilts as you can. If you piece ten or twelve quilts a year, you are bound to get a few really good ones. The rest you can use for backs.
Judy Hopkins, USA

AND THESE, DEAR!

My quilts, at present, are designed in the contemporary style. This enables me to experiment with new possibilities without conforming to traditional format.
Keiko Takahashi, Japan

I belong to a group of six quiltmaking friends. We decided the name for our group would be 'The Well Rounded Quilters'. This seemed like an appropriate title because we are a diverse group. Each of us has a different family situation, we all have varied professional careers and different techniques of quiltmaking appeal to each of us. Of course the best reason for the name is because we all *love* chocolate.

Shelly Burge, USA

Sometimes you travel alone and other times you share the trip with friends. Sometimes you take the back roads and do hand work and other times you feel the need to get on the highway and use your sewing machine. There are often detours and dead ends like running out of fabric, and many times there are wonderful surprises and solutions. But all in all the journey is a delight and your quilts remain as souvenirs of a wonderful journey through the art of quiltmaking.
Carol Doak, USA

Definition of achievement: Spending $55 on fabric before breakfast!
Jenni Dobson, Great Britain

I think that running a quilt show is a lot like being pregnant. You get about six months along, and you think whoa maybe this wasn't such a good idea after all. But there's not much you can do, at that point, except think of a good name.
Claudia Myers, USA

Because distances are so great here in Australia, travelling to teach workshops can be an adventure. Having endured a nightmare, twelve-hour train trip in 37°C (100°F) heat, I vowed to fly next time although I was afraid of small planes. That flight was a 20-seater aircraft; I gulped, confessing to my fellow passenger that I felt as scared as she looked. Imagine my dismay to discover my return flight was a tiny four-seater!

Fifteen years and thousand of kilometres later (and fear long left behind) I now pack my bags in anticipation — flying, like quiltmaking is exhilarating.

Judy Hooworth, Australia

We make quilts like we make our lives — one step at a time — but with quilts we have the option of taking out and reworking the mistakes.
Carter G Houck, USA

KING ARTHUR AND THE KNIGHTS OF THE ROUND QUILT

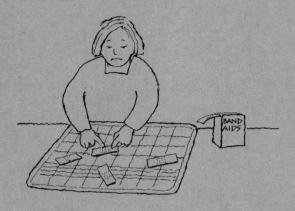

'So much for self-healing'

I gather my inspiration from the earth and from my connections to life in all its forms. I collect colors and patterns and encounters, and I attempt to preserve them in paint and print and text. It is the nature of artists to manipulate nature.
Chris Wolf Edmonds, USA

As a result of the 700th birthday celebration of Switzerland in 1991, my first quilt with a political twist was born. In 1992 I decided to apply for a quilt exhibition in my home country. I therefore sent in two transparencies of my Swiss-cheese-cow quilt. It took the jury quite some time to decide whether or not this bold farce should be accepted. One jury member however was so much in favour of this humorous interpretation that she asked me in earnest prayer to change the title to 'Retrospection of 1991'. According to her statement this was the only way my unusual contribution was going to be accepted. How could I dare do otherwise? The quilt was then sold to an American even before the exhibition had taken place.

Anita Leutwiler, Germany

Being a quiltmaker wrapped up in the fabric of city life creates an inherent paradox that contrasts the traditional image of quiltmaking as part of a simple, make-do, rural way of life with my own complex, urban-shaped space. My workspace in the two bedroom apartment I share with my family is the 40 inch round kitchen table. A long distance view, alternate space, or not making quilts are not options. Until I made quilts, I thought I was creative but not talented. To find something you love to do is a gift. To achieve recognition for it is a miracle. When I am overwhelmed by a longing for functional space complete with a door I can close, I try to remember this.

Paula Nadelstern, USA

Being an art quilter, I continue to push the limits of traditional quiltmaking. In looking at and critiquing the movement of quilting over the last 21 years, I often wonder what our mothers would think of the progress that has taken place, especially with art quilts. Would they be proud of our creativity and techniques? And could they relate to our expression of issues we as women and artists of the twenty-first century face today? Somehow...I think so!

Sara Ann McLennand, USA

Perhaps my most important professional experience happened when I was five years old. I attended kindergarten inside one of the most famous Kyoto temple compounds. Each day I passed through a gate which had doors with different patterns on each side. I never ceased to marvel at this strangely beautiful national treasure, and of course never forgot this experience. Certainly this has provided an important impetus towards the creation of more than 20 reversible log cabin quilts with different but related designs on opposite sides.

Emiko Toda Loeb, USA

I seem to see the world in terms of patchwork and quilting. Continually and instinctively my mind absorbs colours and shapes and arranges things into pattern, fabric, seams and stitching.
Susan Denton, Great Britain

One of my greatest pleasures in designing fabric and quilts is seeing how my work stimulates creativity in others. It is exciting for me to see the wonderful ways quilters add to my designs to create something truly special of their own.
Debbie Mumm, USA

Mother was a hard taskmaster and didn't waste any praise where it wasn't earned. A job that was worth doing was worth doing right and a job well-done was its own reward, a philosophy to which I subscribe.

Although she is no longer physically with me, mother is still looking over my shoulder at every stitch I take and insisting on the removal of any work that is less than my best effort.

Zena Thorpe, USA

On the day of judgement will they count the quilts on the polished floors?
Dorothy Stapleton, Great Britain

If quilters want to be taken seriously, they should learn to take themselves and their work seriously. Next time someone asks you what you do, stand tall and say 'I am a quilter' instead of mumbling 'I do a bit of patchwork'. You will be amazed at the effect it has!
Jill Liddell, Great Britain

The first quilt I remember was one made of my mother's dresses when she was a young school girl — all plaids and prints.
Jane Burch Cochran, USA

When you make a friendship quilt by exchanging fabric, blocks or collaborating with friends on a design or the actual quilt, the quilt exists as a legacy of special friendships that warms the soul as well as the body.
Carol Doak, USA

You can tell an embroiderer from a quilter. An embroiderer delights in creating texture with thread and surface decoration. A quilter will arrange six pieces of fabric next to each other and stroke them. Just stroke them.
Lynne Edwards, Great Britain

As exhibitors at quilt shows, we all know what a dicey business it is to eavesdrop on the comments made by viewers as they can be hurtful as well as pleasing. One of the more amusing ones I've overheard about my work was about my quilt 'Solstice' which is very heavily free-motion machine quilted.

Two ladies came up who although interested in quilts, were clearly non-quilters. Of the two, one was the 'follower' and one was the 'guide' who seemed to know everything about everything. The follower started making admiring remarks about the difficulty of machine quilting. The guide, however, was very quick to put her straight and told her 'Oh, that's no problem. She'll have one of those computerised machines and you just programme in the design and away it goes!'
Barbara Barber, Great Britain

COLUMBUS SETS SAIL FOR AMERICA

Quilts are like people, each has a story to tell.
Gill Turley, Great Britain

Measure twice, cut once.
Adele Corcoran, Great Britain

The images in my wholecloth quilts come directly from my imagination. When I was a child I used to lie in the grass in the summer and watch the clouds until they began to look like faces, or animals, or other pictures. Often quilting develops in much the same way. I look at the painted or patchwork fabric, until a picture develops in my mind. Then I quilt the picture. I like to machine quilt freehand, without following a pencil line. I think of this as doodling with thread. The patterns are as unique and individual to the quilter as handwriting or a signature.

Caryl Bryer Fallert, USA

I grew up with quilts and have loved them from the time I was a little girl. One of my earliest memories is of my mother slipping into my room in the dead of night and covering me gently with yet another quilt to ward off the chill of an unexpected "blue norther". Today I live and work surrounded by beautiful quilts, but nothing has ever provided me with quite the same kind of absolute security, comfort, and sense of being loved that my mama's extra quilt in the night did.

Karey Bresenhan, USA

Good hand quilting is easy — a simple running stitch worked through the three layers of the top, batting and backing. The 'easy' part is down to plenty of practise and a relaxed attitude — give yourself time and don't be unduly critical of your work to begin with — no one starts out as a perfect quilter, it's just down to time and inclination.

Barbara Chainey, Great Britain

When quilting a large quilt, I don't look at the sea of fabric left to be quilted, I focus on the few inches between my hands, and try to make each loop and swirl as beautiful as possible.
Caryl Bryer Fallert, USA

Happiness and inner peace go hand in hand.
Quiltmakers find both in a quiet room with only a quilt
to stitch as their companion! Long may you find this
happiness and inner peace.
Margaret Petit, Great Britain

I heard somewhere about an old quilt in a family being referred to as the 'measles and mumps' quilt. It was so named, because it was placed on the bed when one of the children in the family was ill. The quilt, which was entirely made out of scraps was used as a game by the convalescing child. The idea was to find 'pairs' on the quilt. The possibilities for games and 'stories' are endless and today's quilter has access to the huge variety of fabrics with realistic motifs of every sort and description.
Caroline Wilkinson, Great Britain

Quilting makes my mind race and my blood sing.
Jan Patek, USA

I was tracing my daughters' hands to use as quilting patterns. Their initial confusion about this exercise turned to delight as I explained that someday in the far off future they would place their grown-up hands over the ones I was quilting today and they would remember how their mother had made them each a quilt when they were little girls.
Linda Seward, Great Britain

Beware of eavesdropping. I once ill-advisedly listened to a man who was standing in front of one of my quilts. In a loud, despairing voice he said to his companion 'isn't that horrendous!'
Susan Denton, Great Britain

It is early morning. I am walking along in my beloved city Copenhagen. The light, the shadows from the medieval houses, all the different shapes are like patchwork. The towers and the domes, the fountains, the canals. My city is a quilt.
Lone Holm-Jensen, Denmark

Rule one: Fabric scissors only cut fabric.
Rule two: Always wear a thimble.
Rule three (the most important rule of all): There are no rules in quilting.
Sharon Chambers, Great Britain, *The Quilt Room*

Love, generosity, shared experience. Challenge, perseverance, achievement, colour, pattern, texture. Art, design, geometry and symmetry. Quiltmaking is all these things and more.
Jenny Hutchison, Great Britain

Being a quilter means that you have friends around the world.
Atsuko Ohta, Japan

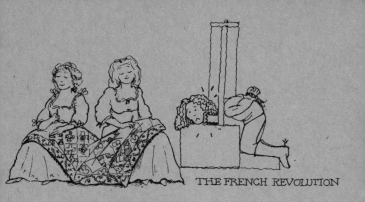

THE FRENCH REVOLUTION

Since the Middle Ages our western culture turned to the abstract, to theory, and written words. Textiles on the contrary still offer touch, warmth and sight. Without words we communicate with a material so familiar to all of us. I am fascinated with this emotional and sensual side of a quilt, a language which all of us understand.
Inge Hueber, Germany

Stitches don't only hold patches of fabric together, they also bind the stitchers into friendships that cross oceans and surround the world.
Jenni Dobson, Great Britain

Quilters make the best friends. Their chosen work demands that they be patient, careful and never stingy with their time — the same qualities flow over into their relationships.
Carter G Houck, USA

In my Fantasy Gallery I wander between quilts, collages and embroideries while music is in the air. Here are no crumpled fabrics, no teasing patterns and no colours faded or run. In a symphony of bright, shining colours the material, form and idea melt into each other in perfect harmony. I like playing with stacks of different colourful fabrics, making them grow together in a process from thought to product. To capture the bright colours in the leaves and the flickering shadows between the branches — is it possible to catch the essence? Can handicraft be made of dreams?

Susanne Birk, Denmark

My dream...After twelve years with quilting classes I got tired and stopped. My idea is to make an old-fashioned quilt and put it in an interior and then paint it in oil — a slow process! I have saved money so I can do this, but during the years I collected old Swedish Quilts. I had to have one quilt exhibition before I started to paint. But I have not been able to start painting yet partly because of 23 exhibitions in Sweden and Paris. The last one was in February 1996 on the Faroe Islands. And I also wrote a book *Old Swedish Quilts*...I still have a dream.
Asa Wettre, Sweden

Who is afraid of silk? Today's silk fabrics are not fragile like the Victorian silks of the nineteenth century. Make use of the exciting structure and texture of the Queen of Fibers. Use the exuberant colours of plain and iridescent silks in quiltmaking, either as small accents or in creating lustrous quilts with only silk fabrics.

Hanne Vibeke de Koning-Stapel, Holland

In many years of quilting, nothing can surpass my joy at seeing my first large quilt hanging in the exhibition in Exeter. I wanted to just stand and stare at it, but felt so shy that I just kept walking past giving it sideways glances.
Linda Negandhi, Great Britain

OF COURSE I'M RELAXED. I'M QUILTING!

I believe that quilts should reflect the stitcher's own background and experience, and hence reflect a flavour different from the usual American or British images most people think of as 'patchwork'. Although I have made many functional bed quilts representing a range of types, I am primarily interested in what has become known as the 'art quilt', the kind that is found on a wall rather than a bed.

Marjorie Coleman, Australia

I am amazed by my generation's fascination with quilts. However, I have come to understand that the attraction is so strong because quilts are so much more than bed covers, and making a quilt involves so much more than just sewing. Quiltmaking is a powerful form of expression, a soothing kind of therapy, and a satisfying, user-friendly creative outlet. My goal is to have each quilt that I make be a product of my heart, as well as my hands.

Judy B Dales, USA

A quilter's idea of a perfect day means having her work all together in a comfy spot, warm enough and light enough. Her favorite music should be playing and the doorbell and telephone should never ring.

Carter G Houck, USA

Two years ago I had cancer and chemotherapy and thanks to the support of my family and my quilting group in Vienna, I'm healthy and full of optimism. During this time, the monthly workshop of the group was 'quilting stitches'. The demonstrator gave a heart motif (I collect everything with hearts) and collected the finished blocks, put them together, stencilled some more hearts on top and presented me with the lovely wallhanging during my next visit. I was very touched and 'my hearts' have a special place in my living-room.
Hanna Afritsch, Austria

How could I have foretold when I saw my first quilt in Pennsylvania, 35 years ago, that patchwork and quilting would become such an important part of my life and that through the craft I would make friends all over the world. I urge quilters everywhere to join a group and make lasting friends.

Jean Roberts, Great Britain, President, *The Quilters' Guild*, 1994–1996

As makers we need to pursue our work of hands, and the intellectual work that governs it, understanding each step of the way that external validation or legitimization is peripheral to the primary business with which we should be involved: the creative dialogue between mind and heart and hand.
Michael James, USA

Quiltmaking is indeed a wonderful experience! It is a symbol of peace and I think it is a unique means that one can express the beauty of mankind.
Keiko Takahashi, Japan

Quilting in Lithuania is just making its first steps. We even had to invent a new word in the Lithuanian language to name quilts. It was registered in the Institute of Lithuanian language and now the word 'skiautiniai' means patchwork quilts ('skiaute' is 'patch' in Lithuanian).
Aldona Tamonyte, Lithuania

A quilt represents time well spent.
Becky Goldsmith, USA

When designing patterns and teaching students, I feel like a composer of music, and await their interpretations to see how they will play my 'songs'. A design is only a beginning. How it will be used is the exciting part. The ingenuity and creativity of quilters continues to amaze me.

Patricia Cox, USA

THIS ONE!

Sitting on the deck of the Nile boat getting through a lock, I sewed my baby blocks! On the pier, an Egyptian watching the boat get down spotted the 'working tourist'. 'What are you doing?' shouted a young man. Displaying the blocks, I talked about quilts. The youth had to translate. The other began to discuss animatedly, I couldn't guess why...and the boat got down...Then, 'from above', the translating go-between shouted down 'My friend here (frantically waving) would like to marry you.' Waving back from 'down under' and thankfully declining, the quilting match eloped with the Nile boat!
Colette Gründisch, Switzerland

The Pitman's Pay
The twilted pettiket so fine,
Frae side to side a fathom stritchin,
A'stitch'd wi'mony a facied line,
Wad stan' itsel', and was bewitchin.
Thomas Wilson

The quilting of a petticoat in those days was a very
important matter, equal to a week's visit from the
tailor's. It was an awful sight to the male inmates of the
house to see the quilting-frame erected on the Monday
morning, with many of the gossips of the vicinity sat
down to their highly important labour. The whole
attention of the mistress was given to these lady-
stitchers; nothing else was properly attended to as long
as this important labour continued. The best of creature
comforts were provided for them, not omitting a drop of
the bottle; for, as they gave their labour without fee or
reward, the choicest fare was expected. Amongst the
improvements of our day, the poor man may thank his
stars that quilted petticoats are no longer in fashion...
Dorothy Osler, Great Britain

Some years ago a quilting friend and I were attending a quilt conference. Enjoying the quilt show we were both struck by a quilt that came into view as we turned a corner. We admired the classic design, exquisite workmanship, and harmonious colour scheme. While still standing near the quilt two more viewers turned the corner and exclaimed, 'What a wonderful quilt — if only they had used different colours'. Confident of our opinion we smiled and walked on with the reminder that beauty is in the eyes of the beholder.

Bettina Havig, USA

My golden rule is think first, take time, be patient, and set high standards.
Gisela Thwaites, Great Britain

BEWARE THE CURSE OF THE MUMMYS'
QUILT!

Quilting has become an international language. At *Le Rouvray* (in the shadow of Notre Dame on the 'left bank' in Paris) quilters from around the world come to visit. We always assure them that it doesn't matter whether they speak French, the Rouvray team speaks patchwork fluently!
Diane de Obaldia, France

So what is this thing called quilting which so engages us all? It is a creative craft that challenges us at all levels, from the simplest block to the art quilt. But it is also a community, a community mostly of women, who through quilting, are able to give a space to themselves. Ostensibly we create quilts for our family, friends, and good causes, but actually the quilts give us a space to express ourselves. We meet for quilting, but through the quilts we find people of a like mind who become friends. Margaret Rolfe, Australia, *Down Under Quilts* 1995

Remember, piecing a quilt is piecing history.
Anon

Ten years ago I was summoned with some urgency, to buy a quilt from a certain Mrs Jones in Cardiganshire, Wales. I purchased a beautiful red and navy flannel pinwheel from her. As I was leaving she burst into floods of tears and began thanking me profusely. I assured her I was as grateful as she. 'No, no, no...' she insisted, this was the money to pay for her funeral! Happily the money continues to accrue interest and I know that on my travels I can always stop by for a cup of tea and a Welsh cake with Mrs Jones.
Jen Jones, Great Britain

In the late seventies, hoping to make an heirloom —
something which would outlive me — I joined a short
course entitled 'An introduction to American quilting'. I
didn't know what American quilting was and had never
seen a quilt. Ever since then quilting has completely
taken over my life. What horrifies me is that if that
course title had included the word patchwork I would
not have touched it with a bargepole!
Edyth Henry, Great Britain

*a little quilt story*
*by*
*Penny Brown*

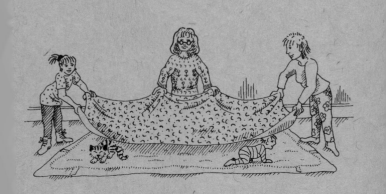

# LIST OF CONTRIBUTORS

Hanna Afritsch
Deidre Amsden

Barbara Barber
Susanne Birk
Georgia J Bonesteel
Colin Brandi
Karey Bresenhan
Penny Brown
Shelly Burge

Barbara Chainey
Sharon Chambers
Gillian Clarke
Annette Claxton
Jane Burch Cochran
Marjorie Coleman
Adele Corcoran
Patricia Cox
Jill Crawley

Judy B Dales
Susan Denton
Carol Doak
Jenni Dobson

Chris Wolf Edmonds
Lynne Edwards
Anny Evason
Caryl Bryer Fallert

Aartha W Greop
Colette Gründisch
Katherine Guerrier

Eliza Calvert Hall
Bettina Havig
Marilyn Henrion
Edyth Henry
Inge Heuber
Jennifer Hollingdale
Lone Holm-Jensen
Judy Hooworth
Judy Hopkins
Carter G Houck
Jenny Hutchison

Michael James
Yoshiko Jinzenji
Nancy Johnson-Srebro
Jen Jones

Helen Kelley
Anita Leutwiler
Jill Liddell
Emiko Toda Loeb

Irene MacWilliam
Sara Ann McLennand
Debbie Mumm
Claudia Myers

Paula Nadelstern
Linda Negandhi
Betsy Nimock

Diane de Obaldia
Atsuko Ohta
Dorothy Osler

Margaret Petit
Jan Patek

Jean Roberts
Margaret Rolfe

Sheila Scawen
Linda Seward
Dorothy Stapleton
Keiko Takahashi
Aldona Tamonyte
Zena Thorpe
Gisela Thwaites
Gill Turley

Meiny Vermaas-van der
Heide
Hanne Vibeke de
Koning-Stapel

Asa Wettre
Caroline Wilkinson

Many thanks to Caroline Wilkinson for compiling the
quotes and to Bonnie Benson of the Quilters' Resource USA
for providing the idea for this book.

The quilts included are from the
Museum Quilts Collection

Published by Museum Quilts (UK) Inc.
254-258 Goswell Road, London EC1V 7EB

Copyright © Museum Quilts Publications, Inc. 1996

Front cover Illustration © Elizabeth Stewart 1996
Illustrations © Elizabeth Stewart 1996
*a little quilt story* Illustrations © Penny Brown 1996

EAN: 5 026285 00166 7

Printed and bound in Hong Kong